RY

science@work
space

COMETS, Stardust, and SUPERNOVAS

By Edward Willett

RSVP ®

RAINTREE
STECK-VAUGHN
PUBLISHERS
A Steck-Vaughn Company

Austin, Texas

www.steck-vaughn.com

Published by Raintree Steck-Vaughn Publishers, an imprint of Steck-Vaughn Company

Library of Congress Cataloging-in-Publication Data

Willett, Edward (Edward Chane) 1959–
    Comets, stardust, and supernovas: the science of space /
by Edward Willett.
       p. cm. — (Science [at] work)
    In ser. statement "[at]" appears as the at symbol.
    Includes bibliographical references and index.
    Summary: An introduction to the study of different aspects
of the solar system and outer space.
    ISBN 0-7398-0134-1
    1. Astronomy—Miscellanea—Juvenile literature. 2. Outer space—
Miscellanea—Juvenile literature. 3. Astronomy—Observers' manuals—
Juvenile literature. [1. Astronomy. 2. Outer space.] I. Title II. Series:
Science [at] work (Austin, Tex.)
QB46.W52   1999
520—DC21   98-47129
                             CIP
                             AC

Printed and bound in Canada
1 2 3 4 5 6 7 8 9 0   03 02 01 00 99

Project Coordinator
Ann Sullivan
Design and Illustration
Warren Clark
Copy Editor
Leslie Strudwick
Layout
Chantelle Sales

Photograph Credits
Every reasonable effort has been made to trace ownership and to obtain permission to reprint copyright material. The publishers would be pleased to have any errors or omissions brought to their attention so that they may be corrected in subsequent printings.

Corel Corporation: pages 4 bottom, 6 left, 8, 9, 11, 13, 14 bottom, 33 top, 39, 42 right; **DigitalVision:** cover top, left, pages 4 middle, 6 top, 8, 16, 22, 32 left, 42 left, 43; **National Aeronautics and Space Administration:** cover bottom right, pages 7, 10, 12, 14 top, 15, 18 top, 19 bottom, 20, 23, 24, 25, 27, 28, 29, 30, 31 top, 32 top, 33 bottom, 34, 35, 38, 40, 41; **Tom Stack and Associates:** page 4 top (Bill and Sally Fletcher), 17 (NASA/TSADO), 18 bottom (Gary Milburn), 19 top (TSADO/NASA), 21 (NASA/GSFC/TSADO), 26 (JPL/TSADO), 31 bottom (Brian Parker), 36 (H. Ford/JHU/ STScl/NASA/TSADO), 37 (Greg Vaughn).

Contents

Have you ever stood outside on a clear night and wondered about the universe?

What are other planets in our solar system like?

How does the Sun work?

Some answers have come from human journeys into space, although the farthest humans have traveled is to the Moon. Some unpiloted spacecraft have traveled to the edge of our solar system. The dream guiding space exploration is that we might someday travel to or make contact with other life in the universe. By learning more about the universe, we also learn more about ourselves and our own planet.

FINDING LINKS

Society

Throughout history, people's questions about space have resulted in many explanations for what they have observed in the sky. Some people once thought stars were souls of the dead. Others thought comets were signs from the gods. Now people use science to find answers to their questions.

Technology

Humans first increased their knowledge about the universe by looking into space from Earth with telescopes and listening to sounds in space with radio antennae. Now people send machines and people into space. Instruments such as the Hubble Space Telescope have helped us see almost as far as the edge of the universe.

The Environment

The Sun and the Moon have many effects on Earth's environment. Ocean tides, the **northern lights**, and life itself are all affected by the Sun and Moon. As we learn more about space, we may discover other events on Earth that are linked to outer space.

Careers

You can learn more about space by becoming a scientist who studies stars and planets. Maybe you can become an astronaut and travel in space.

In Earth's Orbit

"That's one small step for a man, one giant leap for mankind."

—Neil Armstrong, first person to walk on the Moon

For thousands of years, humans have thought Earth was the center of the universe and that everything in the sky revolved around it. But in the last few centuries, we have learned that Earth is just one small planet circling one star, in one solar system, in one galaxy. Our galaxy is just one of millions of galaxies in the universe.

Of all the billions of points of light in the sky, only the Moon orbits Earth—about once every 28 days. Using just the eye, people can see the Moon better than any other object in space. This explains why for centuries people have written poems and songs about the Moon.

What is the Moon made of?

When you look at the Moon, you can see it does not all look the same. It has dark spots and lighter spots. This pattern has made people sometimes say the Moon is made of strange things, like green cheese. It is really made of rocks, very much like the rocks on Earth. The dark parts are low, relatively level areas covered with layers of a dark rock called **basalt**. They were formed when huge pools of lava slowly cooled. The lighter areas are higher, more rugged regions. They are made of many different types of lighter-colored rocks.

Like Earth, the Moon is covered with soil. Moon soil is made of broken-up rubble and powder that can be anywhere from 3 to 65 feet (1 to 20 m) deep. On Earth, soil forms as wind and water wear rock away over thousands of years. On the Moon, where there is no air, soil has been created by **meteorites** crashing into and shattering the Moon's surface. Meteorites range in size from tiny specks of dust to large **asteroids** that have blasted out craters in the Moon's surface that are many miles across.

Moon rocks like this one are formed from hardened lava. They contain greater amounts of calcium, aluminum, and titanium than most Earth rocks.

BYTE-SIZED FACT

Before people explored the Moon, scientists had three theories about its origin. One theory was that it used to be part of Earth. Another was that it formed near Earth. The third theory was that it formed somewhere else, floated by in space, and was captured by Earth's gravity. Because of differences between Earth rocks and Moon rocks, most scientists do not think the Moon was ever part of Earth. We may never know exactly where or how it was formed.

How does the Moon orbit Earth?

The Moon is Earth's natural satellite. A satellite is any object that orbits another object in space.

To understand how orbiting works, think about it in terms of a baseball traveling through the air. If you throw a baseball as hard as you can, it will travel a long way, but it will eventually fall to the ground because of gravity. If you could throw the ball harder, it would travel farther, but it would still fall. However, if you could throw the baseball really, really fast— 17,800 miles per hour (28,500 kph)—not only would you be the greatest baseball pitcher of all time, but your baseball would start orbiting Earth. The baseball would be moving so fast that Earth's rounded surface would curve away from the ball at the same rate that gravity pulls it down. As long as the ball kept moving at 17,800 miles per hour (28,500 kph), it would remain in orbit, and would never hit the ground. As a result, it would just keep going around the planet.

Earth's gravity keeps fast-moving objects from flying out into space. This is how the Moon and human-made satellites stay in orbit around Earth.

Ocean Tides

Have you ever been at a beach near the ocean and noticed that sometimes the water comes up farther than other times?

The Moon creates this change by causing ocean tides. The Moon's gravity pulls all the water on Earth toward it, making the water deeper on the side of the planet facing the Moon and on the side directly opposite. But since Earth is constantly spinning, this area of high water changes. As a coastline passes into the area of low tide, the water creeps up the shore, and we say the tide comes in. As the coastline moves out from under this area, the water level falls, and we say the tide has gone out. The Sun's gravity also influences the tides. Even though it is much bigger than the Moon, its effect on tides is smaller because it is so far away from Earth.

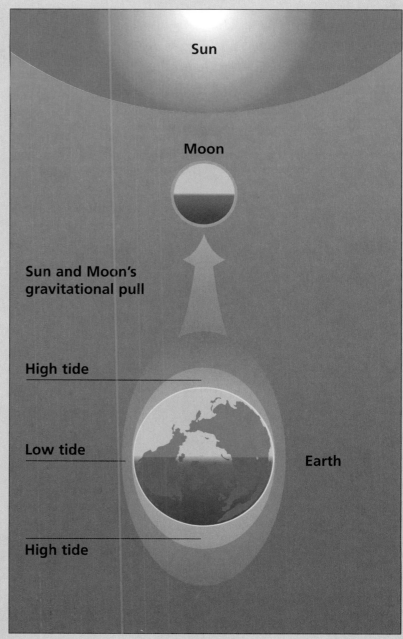

Sun

Moon

Sun and Moon's gravitational pull

High tide

Low tide

Earth

High tide

When there is high tide on one side of Earth, there is high tide on the opposite side as well. As Earth rotates, shorelines move into the areas of high and low tides.

What other objects orbit Earth?

Artificial satellites, which are human-made objects, orbit Earth along with the Moon. The Union of Soviet Socialist Republics (U.S.S.R.) launched the first artificial satellite, *Sputnik 1*, in 1957. The U.S. launched its first satellite, *Explorer 1*, in 1958. Today thousands of satellites orbit Earth and perform many useful tasks.

Types of Satellites

Communications satellites allow radio and television signals to be transmitted around the globe. Most of the television you watch has bounced off a satellite. Scientific research satellites study space. Navigational satellites send out radio signals that help people on the ground or at sea pinpoint their exact location on Earth. Reconnaissance satellites help the military track the movements of troops and ships and detect missile launches. Weather satellites watch Earth and help people predict the weather more accurately. These satellites have saved thousands of lives by helping to track hurricanes and other violent storms. Land and sea observation satellites study Earth. These satellites help scientists learn how to protect the environment better.

The *Explorer I* was launched on January 31, 1958 by the Jupiter-C vehicle.

The two bowl-shaped parts of this communications satellite receive and transmit signals from one place on Earth to another.

How does a rocket work?

Rockets are the only method humans have right now of putting objects into space. The first trip to the Moon, and the first satellites, would have been impossible without rocket technology.

It takes a lot of energy to overcome Earth's gravity. Rockets provide that energy. In a rocket, fuel and an **oxidizer** burn together. The oxidizer is important because it provides an important source of oxygen. On Earth, there is oxygen all around us, but there is no oxygen in space. Rockets are able to work in space because they carry their own oxygen with them.

Burning the fuel produces hot gases, which are discharged through a nozzle. As the great scientist Sir Isaac Newton discovered, "For every action there is an equal and opposite reaction." In a rocket, that means that when the hot gases rush out of the nozzle, an equal force pushes the rocket in the opposite direction. The rocket does not fly by "pushing" its exhaust against the ground or the air. It does not matter whether a rocket is on the ground, in the air, or in space. As long as exhaust is rushing out of the rocket in one direction, the rocket will move in the other direction.

The force of the exhaust going in one direction causes the rocket to move in the opposite direction.

BYTE-SIZED FACT

Rockets were invented in China some time before the 13th century for fireworks and warfare. It was not until 1883 that a Russian schoolteacher, Konstantin Tsiolkovsky, realized that rockets would work in a **vacuum** and could be used for space travel.

Race to the Moon

In the late 1950s and early 1960s, the United States and the U.S.S.R were locked in a "space race."

Both countries were trying to be the first to explore space. On April 12, 1961, Colonel Yuri Gagarin, a Russian fighter pilot, became the first person to orbit Earth in *Vostok I*.

After Gagarin's flight, President John F. Kennedy vowed that the United States would land a man on the Moon by the end of the decade. On July 20, 1969, Neil Armstrong became the first person to walk on the Moon. His mission, *Apollo 11*, was launched by the most powerful rocket ever built, the *Saturn V*, which was as tall as a 30-story building.

Millions of people watched the landing on live television. As he stepped onto the Moon's surface, Armstrong said, "That's one small step for a man, one

The American flag is still "waving" on the surface of the Moon today.

giant leap for mankind." Armstrong and a fellow astronaut, Edwin "Buzz" Aldrin, spent more than 2 hours on the surface, inspecting the spacecraft, placing scientific equipment, and gathering rock samples. They even planted an American flag, stiffened with wire to look like it was waving in the breeze.

BYTE-SIZED FACT

Six more Apollo missions went to the Moon after *Apollo 11*. Only 5 of them landed because an explosion on *Apollo 13* forced it to return to Earth. The last Apollo flight, *Apollo 17*, was in 1972. No one has been to the Moon since.

Saturn V

The *Saturn V* rocket had three parts that helped the astronauts get to the Moon:

- A cone-shaped command module nicknamed "Columbia," in which the three astronauts on the mission rode

- A cylinder-shaped service module, containing a rocket motor and fuel

- A lunar excursion module (LEM) nicknamed "Eagle." The Eagle was the only part of *Saturn V* that actually landed on the Moon.

What is it like to ride on the Space Shuttle?

On the launchpad, you lie on your back with your feet up. In your mind, you run through everything you have learned through months and years of training to be an astronaut. You feel ready for any emergency.

When the countdown reaches T minus 6 seconds, the shuttle's three liquid rocket engines start. Outside there is an ear-splitting roar, but inside

It takes a great deal of fuel to launch an object as large and as heavy as the Space Shuttle away from the pull of Earth's gravity.

Astronauts must know how to use all of the instruments in the shuttle.

you cannot hear anything. However, you can feel the shuttle shaking and swaying back and forth.

The count reaches zero, and a voice on your helmet radio says, "SRB Ignition—Liftoff!" Your shuttle's two solid rocket boosters ignite. The shuttle moves upward. The whole crew cabin rattles and shakes even more. You feel yourself being pushed back in your seat about as much as you do on a jet airplane during takeoff.

Two minutes after liftoff, the solid rocket boosters burn out and fall away,

which makes the ride smoother. Three liquid-fueled rockets continue to burn. Since the shuttle has lost the solid rockets and is using up fuel, it is getting lighter and going faster.

By 7.5 minutes into the flight, the shuttle weighs only one-tenth what it did at launch, and you feel like you weigh three times as much as you do on Earth, making it hard to even breathe. At this point the engines are throttled down so the acceleration does not increase, and the astronauts do not feel any heavier.

Finally, the main engines cut off. The thrust stops, and you suddenly find yourself weightless. You are in space!

Shuttle Astronaut

How can you become a shuttle astronaut?

It is important that you are physically fit. You also must have the right education. Mission specialists and pilots must have at least a bachelor's degree in engineering, science, or mathematics. A master's or doctorate is even better. You must also have three years of related experience. If you want to be a shuttle pilot, you have to learn to fly jets first. Pilots must have at least 1,000 hours of experience flying jets, and they must have perfect vision.

Finally, you have to apply for the shuttle astronaut program. For more information, write to the Astronaut Selection Office, NASA Johnson Space Center, Houston, TX 77058.

BYTE-SIZED FACT

On average, more than 4,000 people apply for the approximately 20 openings for shuttle astronauts that become available every 2 years.

Dr. Chiaki Mukai moves from the Space Shuttle *Columbia*'s cabin to the cargo bay through this tunnel.

Astronauts go on a "space walk" to repair equipment on the outside of the Space Shuttle.

What is a space station?

A space station is a permanent, orbiting structure in which people can live. Scientists have been talking about space stations for as long as they have been talking about exploring space. The first American space station was *Skylab*. Three, three-person crews spent a total of 172 days there in 1973 and 1974. It later fell out of orbit and landed in Australia.

The Russians launched their own space station, *Mir*, in February 1986. Astronauts from the United States started visiting *Mir*. Russian cosmonauts and American astronauts have lived on *Mir* for months at a time.

Starting in 1999, a new space station, the *International Space Station*, will be built. Once it is finished, people from many different countries will live in it year-round to study how living in space affects humans. This knowledge will be needed if people ever travel to Mars or other planets. Other important research will focus on using

A solar shield was deployed by the second crew of *Skylab* to shade its Orbital Workshop (OWS).

space to make new materials or medicines that cannot be made on Earth. *The International Space Station* is a joint project of NASA, the European Space Agency (which represents Belgium, France, Germany, Italy, the Netherlands, the United Kingdom, Denmark, Spain, Sweden, Switzerland, Ireland, Austria, Norway, and Finland), Russia, Canada, Japan, Italy, and Brazil.

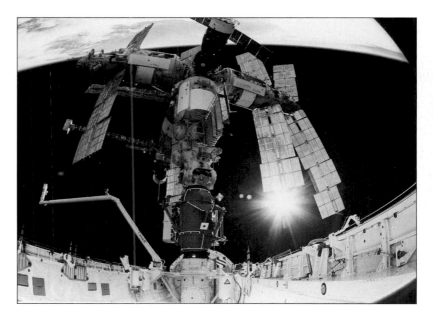

In 1995 Space Station *Mir* docked with the Space Shuttle *Atlantis*.

In the Sun's Orbit

"Even during an eclipse, you should never look directly at the Sun."

The Sun, while much farther from Earth than the Moon, is very important to our planet. Without heat from the Sun, Earth would be a frozen rock without plants, animals, or people. The Sun is at the center of our solar system. This solar system includes Earth and eight other planets. Just as the Moon orbits Earth, Earth and the other planets orbit the Sun.

What is the Sun?

The Sun is an enormous ball of extremely hot gases, more than 100 times as large as Earth. The Sun is very far away—93 million miles (149 million km)—which is a good thing, because its surface is so hot. It is more than 100 times hotter than the hottest day in the hottest desert on Earth. Inside the Sun, the temperature is even hotter, an incredible 27 million°F (15 million°C)!

The Sun is a star. It looks different from the other stars in the sky because it is so much closer to Earth than any other star. Amazingly, some stars in the universe are as much as five times hotter than our Sun.

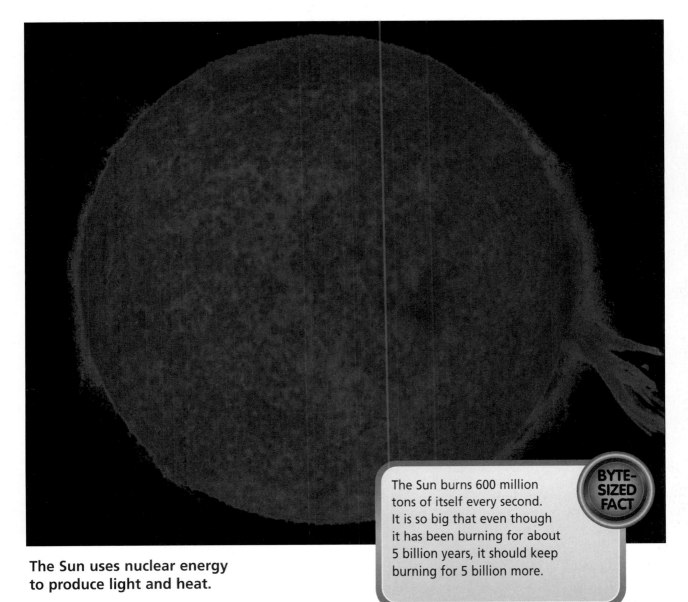

The Sun uses nuclear energy to produce light and heat.

BYTE-SIZED FACT

The Sun burns 600 million tons of itself every second. It is so big that even though it has been burning for about 5 billion years, it should keep burning for 5 billion more.

The Telescope

A telescope is a device that makes objects that are far away look closer.

Hans Lippershey of Holland invented the telescope in 1608, but Italian scientist Galileo

BYTE-SIZED FACT

Earth's **atmosphere** is difficult to see through because the air is constantly moving. That movement makes the stars appear to twinkle. Scientists have tried to observe stars without the twinkling by putting a telescope in space, above the atmosphere. The Hubble Space Telescope is a reflector telescope with a mirror 8 feet (2.4 m) across. It was launched by a Space Shuttle in 1990. Improvements were made to it in 1993 and 1997, and more improvements are planned. The telescope will keep working until at least 2005. The Hubble Space Telescope has helped us learn more about the births of stars and galaxies, **black holes**, our own solar system, and the existence of planets around other stars.

Galilei was the first person to use a telescope to study space. Though his telescopes could only magnify objects less than 30 times their actual size, Galileo discovered mountains on the Moon, Jupiter's four brightest moons, the **phases** of the planet Venus, and the stars of our galaxy.

There are two main kinds of telescopes. The refractor, the kind Galileo used, is a series of

The Hubble Space Telescope is used to gather valuable information about a variety of space objects. It sends images of planets, stars, galaxies, and other things back to Earth for astronomers to study.

lenses that collect and magnify light rays from a distant object. The reflector, demonstrated by Sir Isaac Newton in 1668, collects light with a mirror shaped like a shallow bowl. The largest refractor telescope was built in 1879 near Chicago. It has a lens more than 3 feet (1 m) in diameter. The largest reflector, located in Russia, has a mirror more than 20 feet (6 m) across.

Astronomers use powerful telescopes like this one to explore space without leaving Earth.

What are sunspots?

Sunspots were discovered by Galileo, who risked going blind by looking at the Sun through his telescope. He saw dark blotches that slowly moved across the Sun's surface and changed from week to week. For a long time, nobody knew what sunspots were.

Although scientists do not know everything about sunspots, they know they are not really black. Sunspots just appear black because they are much cooler than the rest of the Sun, which appears orange. Researchers also know that sunspots have very strong **magnetic fields**. Sunspot activity follows a regular 11-year cycle, going from a period with no or few sunspots to one with many sunspots. The sunspot cycle may affect Earth's climate. When sunspots peak, for instance, the southeastern United States seems to experience colder-than-normal temperatures. Sunspots are associated with solar flares. Solar flares are huge explosions on the Sun's surface. They occur in regions around the sunspots.

A close-up view of a sunspot

It is dangerous under any circumstances to look directly at the Sun, with or without a telescope.

Solar flares sometimes cause problems on Earth. They can interfere with satellites and even cause power blackouts. A solar flare in March 1989 blacked out the entire Canadian province of Quebec and created huge northern lights that were seen as far south as the Caribbean.

BYTE-SIZED FACT

What is solar wind?

The Sun sends out energy in all directions. Only two-billionths of this energy hits Earth, but that is enough to keep the planet warm. Without the Sun, even the air on Earth would be frozen solid.

The Sun also sends out more than 1 million tons of gas particles per second. These particles are the **solar wind**. The solar wind takes about 10 days to pass by Earth. By the time it does, it is spread so thinly that there are only about 80 particles of it in each cubic inch (5 particles in each cubic centimeter) of space.

The solar wind is what causes the northern (and southern) lights. Earth's magnetic field makes the solar wind particles zoom toward the poles, where they collide with oxygen and nitrogen **atoms** in the upper atmosphere. Oxygen atoms glow green, and nitrogen atoms glow red, making a colorful pattern appear to move across the sky.

This set of southern lights, or *Aurora Australis*, appears halfway between Australia and Antarctica.

Sun and Earth

The Sun can be harmful as well as helpful.

In addition to heat and light, the Sun sends out **ultraviolet** radiation. This radiation can damage human skin, causing sunburns. Too much of it may eventually cause skin cancer. Wearing sunscreen can protect you from these damaging rays.

Earth has its own sunscreen, a thin layer of gas called **ozone**, high in the atmosphere. Ozone blocks out much of the Sun's ultraviolet radiation. In recent years, however, this layer has become thinner. Certain chemicals that humans use in items such as refrigerators and air conditioners have escaped into the air and eaten away at the ozone layer. Many countries are working together to get rid of these chemicals and protect the ozone layer.

This computer-enhanced photo of the ozone layer shows the hole in it.

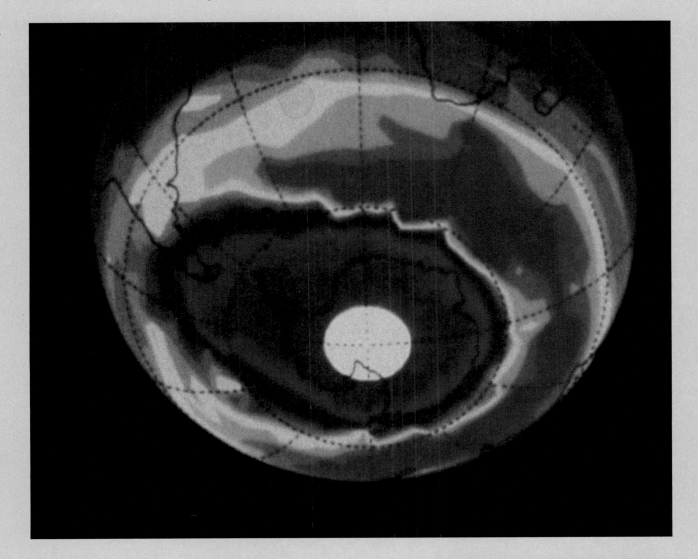

What are planets?

When human beings first started looking at the stars, they noticed that although most of the stars stayed in the same spot relative to one another, some kept changing their position. Ancient astronomers called these objects "wanderers." We now know that they are not stars at all, and we call them planets. Planets are huge spheres of rock or gas circling a star. Some of them are smaller than Earth; some are much larger.

Most of the planets we know orbit our own Sun. With Earth, these planets form our solar system. Recently, scientists have discovered planets orbiting other stars. This probably means that many of the stars we see in the night sky are at the center of their own solar systems of planets and moons.

BYTE-SIZED FACT

The planets from the closest to the Sun to the one farthest away are Mercury, Venus, Earth, Mars, Jupiter, Saturn, Uranus, Neptune, and Pluto. A good way to remember the order of planets is by remembering the phrase, "Mark very eagerly made a jelly sandwich under no protest." The first letter of each word is the first letter of each planet. The "a" stands for "asteroids." Asteroids are rocky objects that orbit the Sun between Mars and Jupiter. Asteroids have diameters of less than 620 miles (1,000 km).

What is Mercury like?

Mercury is the closest planet to the Sun, so during the day it is extremely hot. However, at night it is three times colder than the coldest temperature ever recorded on Earth. Mercury looks like Earth's moon, with craters, lava flows, and dust-covered hills and plains. It is about one-third Earth's size, but has no atmosphere. Unlike Earth and most of the other planets, it has no moon of its own. If you lived on Mercury, you would not see very many sunrises and sunsets. Mercury's day, the time it takes to spin completely around its **axis** once, is about two Earth months long!

When a spacecraft took this photograph of Mercury's South Pole, it was 53,200 miles (85,800 km) away.

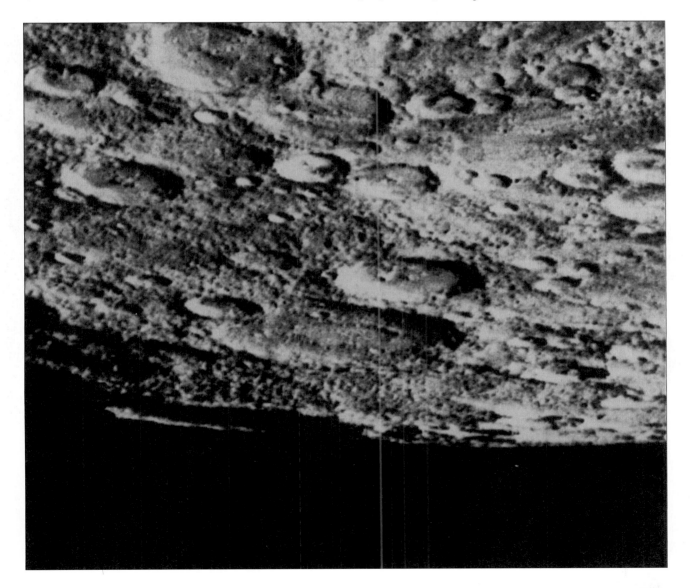

What is Venus like?

It is hard to see the surface of Venus because the planet is constantly covered with clouds. These clouds reflect light very well, which is why Venus is the brightest object in the sky except for the Moon. Science fiction writers used to imagine that beneath its clouds, Venus was covered with huge oceans and jungles. However, today scientists know that its atmosphere is mostly carbon dioxide. This gas traps heat from the Sun, making Venus's surface extremely hot. Venus is almost the same size as Earth, but its day is even longer than Mercury's—a Venusian day is almost eight Earth months long.

BYTE-SIZED FACT

Venus is the first planet that a spacecraft from Earth touched down on. The Union of Soviet Socialist Republic's *Venera 3* probe landed on the planet in 1966. The U.S.S.R. went on to land several more probes on the planet. These probes quickly discovered that the surface temperature is hot enough to melt lead! They also found out that Venus's beautiful white clouds are made of corrosive **sulfuric acid**.

Venus has a number of mountains on its surface. Sapas, Maat, and Ozza are visible in this picture.

What is Mars like?

Astronomers in the 19th century thought they saw straight lines that were canals on the surface of Mars. For many years people thought there was life on Mars. Spacecraft that have since visited Mars, however, have shown that nothing is living on the planet.

Although Mars, like Venus, has a carbon dioxide atmosphere, Mars's atmosphere is much thinner, with a pressure 150 times less than that of Earth. Although it can reach 80°F (27°C) at the equator, Mars is mostly very cold, with an average temperature of about -40°F (-40°C). Mars is only

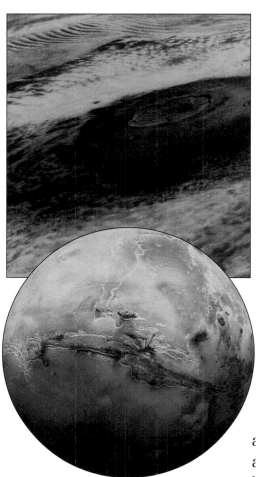

From a distance of 1,500 miles (2,500 km), Valles Marineris canyon can be seen in the center of Mars.

Olympus Mons is the largest volcano in our solar system.

a little more than half as big as Earth, but its day is almost exactly the same length, lasting 24 hours and 37 minutes. It has two small, rocky moons called Phobos and Deimos.

Mars would be an interesting place to visit. You could go sightseeing at the solar system's largest volcano, Olympus Mons. This volcano is 16 miles (25 km) tall—almost three times as tall as Mount Everest, the highest mountain on Earth. Or you could stop by one of the solar system's largest canyons, Valles Marineris canyon, which is almost 4 miles (6 km) deep—more than three times as deep as the Grand Canyon. You would have to watch for giant, planet-wide dust storms that could ruin your whole vacation!

Mars Exploration

American spacecraft	Mission	Year
U.S. Mariner IX	orbited Mars	1971, 1972
Viking I	released landing vehicles	1976
Mars Sojourner	landed on Mars	1997

Asteroids

Asteroids are rocky or metallic objects that orbit the Sun, but they are too small to be planets.

They range from the size of a pebble to 620 miles (1,000 km) in diameter. Most are found between the orbits of Mars and Jupiter, but they can turn up anywhere in the solar system. Asteroids were once thought to be the pieces of a shattered planet, but today most scientists think they are raw materials that failed to form into a planet.

An asteroid on a collision course with Earth is called a **meteor**. Most burn up in the atmosphere. If they reach the ground, they are called meteorites. Small meteorites have dented cars and smashed holes in the roofs of houses. Large meteorites are much more dangerous, however. Earth's chances of a major asteroid impact in the next century are estimated to be about one in 10,000.

Although it appears small, this asteroid is approximately 32 miles (51 km) long.

BYTE-SIZED FACT

In 1908 something from space, probably about the size of a house, hit the atmosphere above the Tunguska Forest in Siberia and exploded. Hundreds of square miles of forest were burned, and thousands of square miles more were knocked down. Many scientists believe a large meteorite that hit the Yucatan Peninsula in Mexico about 65 million years ago may have caused the extinction of dinosaurs.

Meteorite Damage

Diameter	Damage
0.4 miles (0.6 km)	On land, would cause earthquakes and fires over an area between 400 and 4,000 square miles (1,000 and 10,000 sq km)
	In the ocean, would create a huge wave that could flood surrounding coastlines up to 0.6 miles (1 km) inland
1 mile (1.6 km)	Would cool off the entire planet by sending water vapor and dust into the atmosphere
	Would block much of the Sun's energy and would damage the ozone layer
1.9 miles (3 km)	Could completely destroy the ozone layer and cause a new ice age
6 miles (9.6 km)	Would explode with a force 10,000 times greater than all the nuclear weapons in the world going off at once
	Would cause earthquakes, turn the air burning hot, and make the Sun disappear for a year, wiping out millions of plant and animal species

What is Jupiter like?

Jupiter is the largest planet in the solar system, more than 11 times as big as Earth. It is mainly made up of hydrogen and helium. It has no solid surface at all. No one is sure why, but Jupiter puts out more heat than it receives from the Sun. Most people think Saturn is the only planet with a ring around it, but Jupiter has a ring, too. However, Jupiter's ring is made of rocky particles so small that we cannot see the ring from Earth. Jupiter has 16 moons that we know of. Jupiter also boasts the biggest and longest-lasting storm in the solar system. The Great Red Spot, which has been in existence for centuries, is a storm similar to a hurricane. This hurricane is bigger than Earth!

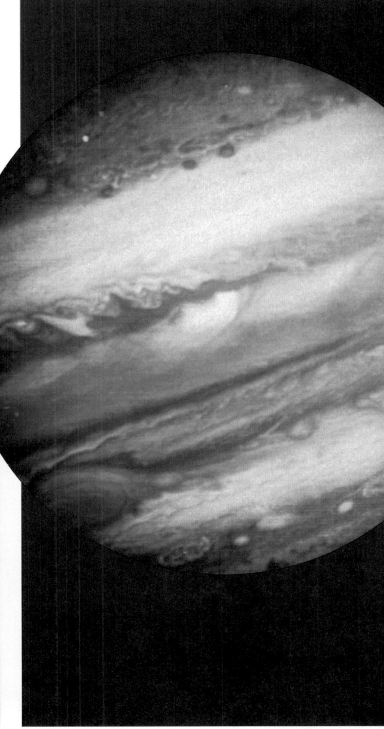

Jupiter's Great Red Spot is really a giant storm.

The colorful bands on Jupiter are caused by weather patterns in its atmosphere.

What are Saturn and Uranus like?

Saturn is best known for its rings, which can be seen from Earth. They are made of particles ranging from tiny specks of dust to icy chunks many feet wide. Like Jupiter, Saturn is made of gas, and it gives off more heat than it receives. Saturn has at least 21 moons, which is more than any other planet in the solar system. It is slightly smaller than Jupiter, but still almost ten times bigger than Earth.

Like Saturn, Uranus has rings. Its rings are made of large, rocky chunks. It has almost as many moons as Jupiter—at least 15. The atmosphere on Uranus is much colder than that of Jupiter or Saturn. Uranus is also much smaller than Jupiter or Saturn, but it is still more than four times bigger than Earth.

The Hubble Space Telescope has taken hundreds of photographs. This one shows a rare storm at the center of the planet. This storm is about the same size as Earth—about 7,900 miles (12,700 km) across!

Voyager II flew past Uranus in 1985.

A space probe is traveling to Saturn right now. *Cassini*, launched by the United States in 1997, is scheduled to reach Saturn in June 2004.

BYTE-SIZED FACT

What is Neptune like?

Neptune's atmosphere is blue because it contains a great deal of **methane**. Like Jupiter, it has a huge, permanent, hurricane-like storm. Neptune's storm, called the Great Dark Spot, is as big as Earth. Like the other big gas planets, Neptune has rings and at least eight moons.

Even though it is farther away from the Sun than Uranus, Neptune is warmer. Like Jupiter and Saturn, it puts out more heat than it gets from the Sun. Neptune is slightly smaller than Uranus.

Triton is Neptune's largest moon.

Wispy white clouds sometimes cover Neptune's Great Dark Spot.

BYTE-SIZED FACT

The only close-up pictures of Uranus and Neptune that exist were taken by the *Voyager II* spacecraft, which was never intended to go to those planets at all! *Voyager II* was supposed to go to Jupiter and Saturn. But after *Voyager I* showed that Saturn's moon Titan was covered with clouds and could not be photographed very well, NASA decided to send *Voyager II* on to Uranus and Neptune. *Voyager II* was only given a 30 percent chance of reaching either planet, but in 1986 it sent back pictures of Uranus, and in 1989 pictures of Neptune. It then traveled beyond our solar system.

What is Pluto like?

Pluto is usually thought of as the planet farthest from the Sun. Although it averages 3.7 billion miles (5.9 billion km) from the Sun during its orbit, for years at a time it is actually closer to the Sun than Neptune. Because it is so far away from the center of the solar system, Pluto takes a long time to orbit the Sun—248 years. Pluto is about one-fourth the size of Earth and has a moon, Charon, that is one-third as large as it. Both Pluto and Charon seem to be made of frozen water, ammonia, and methane. Scientists believe Pluto is pale blue because it has a crust of frozen methane. When Pluto was at its closest point to the Sun, in 1989, some of the methane thawed, giving the planet a fairly large atmosphere. Most of the time it has none at all.

Pluto, shown on the left, is about 39 times farther away from the Sun than Earth. Its moon, Charon, shown on the right, was discovered by astronomers in 1978.

BYTE-SIZED FACT

Comets are bits of frozen gases, water, ice, and dust that orbit the Sun even farther out than Pluto. Occasionally a comet gets drawn into the inner solar system by gravity. It begins to heat up as it nears the Sun. The frozen gases and ice begin to boil, surrounding the comet with a cloud of gas and dust as big as a planet. This is called the coma. Pressure from the solar wind causes the coma to stretch out behind the comet like a long tail, sometimes tens of millions of miles long. Sometimes comets come close enough to Earth that this tail can be seen clearly.

Is there life on other planets?

Three things are necessary for life: chemicals called **organic compounds**, liquid water, and a source of energy. We know of only two places in the solar system that have or have had all three—Earth and Mars. However, Jupiter's moon Europa may have all three as well. The spacecraft *Galileo* took photographs of Europa's ice-covered surface that seemed to show places where liquid water has welled out of cracks. That means Europa may have a huge underground ocean. As a result, many scientists believe Europa is the most likely place in the solar system, other than Earth, where life might exist.

Mars probably does not have any life now, but it may have once. Mars is bone-dry, but it used to have lots of water. A meteorite from Mars found in Antarctica contained traces of elements that could have come from ancient living things.

Humans may never be able to visit planets around other stars, but they continue to hope to find other intelligent life in the universe. For now, the only way we can search is by listening. Earth constantly sends radio and television signals into space. Other worlds may be doing the same. By scanning the sky with radio telescopes, scientists hope they might eventually hear a signal from some other solar system.

Jupiter's moon Europa may have the elements needed to sustain life.

This field of radio telescopes is always listening for signals from distant planets and galaxies.

In Deep Space

"To boldly go
where no one
has gone before."
—*Star Trek: The Next
Generation*

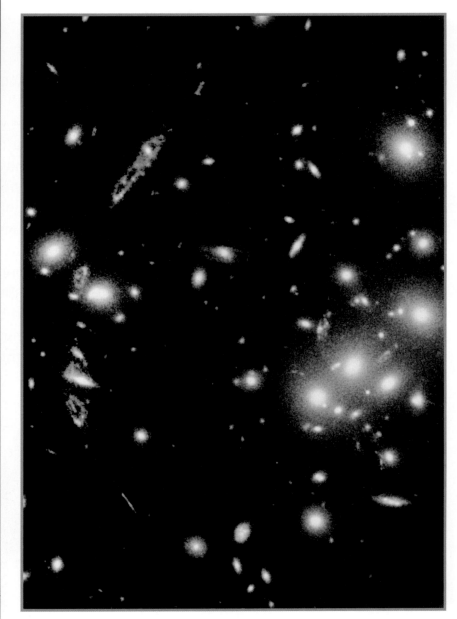

The solar system is big compared to Earth, but it is tiny compared to the universe as a whole. When we look up at the night sky, we can only see a small portion of the universe. What we see mainly are the tiny, twinkling lights we call stars. It can be hard to believe just how far away and how big those tiny lights really are. For a long time, people believed stars were merely lamps hung from the arch of heaven.

How did the universe begin? How will it end?

Scientists think the universe started with a Big Bang—an enormous explosion—between 11 billion and 20 billion years ago. They believe the universe has been getting bigger ever since. Some scientists predict that one of two things will happen to the universe in the future. It will either continue to expand, or it will collapse. The occurrence of either of these events depends on the total **mass** of the universe. Every object in the universe has mass, and every object with mass has gravity. All objects with gravity attract one another. This means that if there is enough mass, the universe has enough gravity to eventually stop itself from expanding and start contracting.

If there is not enough mass, the universe will expand forever. Scientists who have added together the mass of all the galaxies and stars we can see believe there is not enough mass to make the universe collapse. However, scientists believe the universe contains invisible **matter**, called "dark matter," that might give the universe enough mass to keep it from expanding. Nobody is sure what dark matter is or if it exists. It could be ordinary matter we cannot see, or something very strange we have never come across before.

If the universe began with a Big Bang, matter and energy would have been thrown in all directions.

Astronomers believe that this group of three galaxies and the cloud of hot gas are surrounded by "dark matter" that cannot be seen or detected.

What are stars?

Just like the Sun, stars are balls of hot gas. Most are tens or hundreds of times bigger than Earth. Even though the night sky seems to be filled with stars, only a few thousand can be seen with the human eye.

Even the nearest stars are very far away. The distance to the stars is measured in **light years**. One light year is the distance light travels in a year. Since the speed of light is 186,000 miles (300,000 km) per second, one light year is almost 6 trillion miles (10 trillion km)! Next to the Sun, our nearest star, Proxima Centauri, is a little more than 3.5 light years away. Proxima Centauri is visible only south of the equator.

This photograph, taken by the Hubble Space Telescope, shows almost 10,000 stars in two giant star clusters. That is more than twice as many stars as can be seen with the naked eye on a clear night on Earth.

BYTE-SIZED FACT

When you look at a star, you are really seeing the way it looked many years ago, when the light you see started its journey to Earth. Looking into the night sky is like looking back in time, sometimes hundreds or even thousands of years.

What are galaxies?

Galaxies are collections of tens of millions of stars. Our galaxy, called the Milky Way, has billions of stars in it, but the Milky Way is only one of millions upon millions of galaxies in the universe. That means there are more than a trillion stars in the universe—that is a one with 18 zeros after it!

Galaxies come in a variety of shapes. The Milky Way is a spiral galaxy—it is shaped like water going down a drain. Spiral galaxies are the most common, but some are oval-shaped, some are circular, and some have unique shapes. Galaxies form groups called clusters.

M31, or the Andromeda galaxy, is 2 million light years away from Earth!

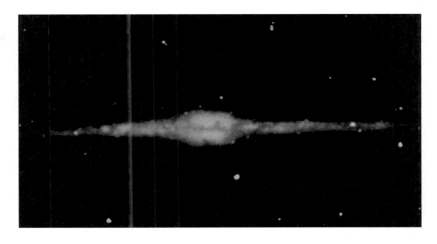

Our solar system is located in this spiral galaxy, the Milky Way.

Our galaxy belongs to a cluster called the Local Group, which has about 30 galaxies in it. Many of these are very small; some of them orbit around the Milky Way. The Milky Way is the second-largest galaxy in the Local Group. The largest is M31, called the Andromeda Galaxy because it is found in the constellation Andromeda.

It contains 300 billion stars.

BYTE-SIZED FACT

Sometimes galaxies run into each other, but the stars are so far apart they rarely collide. However, the dust clouds in two galaxies may collide, sending out shock waves that can damage stars in both galaxies.

What is a black hole?

When a star collapses, it sometimes turns into a black hole. A black hole has gravity so strong that nothing, not even light, can break free from it. All objects in the universe, even people, have gravity. The more mass an object has, the more gravity it has. Individual people do not have much gravity because they do not have much mass. Earth's much greater gravity floods human gravity.

Earth's gravity, in turn, is nothing compared to the gravity of the Sun, which holds the whole solar system in orbit. But even the Sun's gravity is not strong enough to prevent light from escaping. If the Sun was much smaller, only 4 miles (6 km) across instead of 875,000 miles (1.4 million km), and its mass was the same, its gravity would be strong enough to stop light from escaping, and it would be a black hole.

No one has ever seen a black hole, but scientists believe they have seen the effects of black holes in a number of places in the sky.

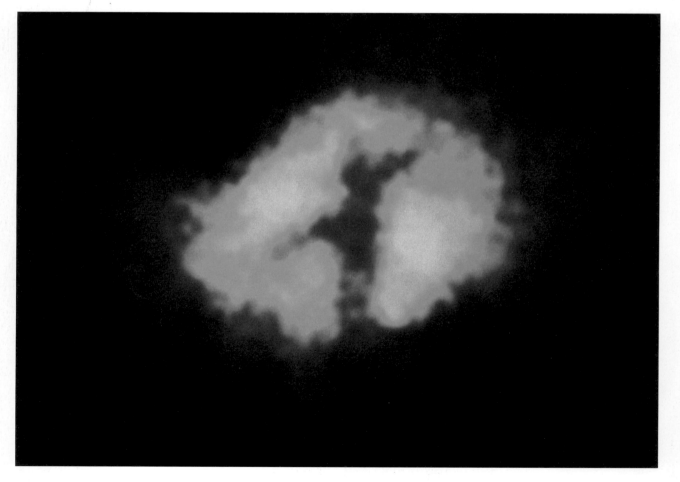

This black hole is in the center of the M51 galaxy.

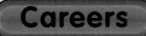
Astronomer

An astronomer is a scientist who studies outer space and the objects found there.

To be an astronomer, you need to be good at math and able to think logically. You also have to be able to use a computer. Astronomers are very patient and determined. They often spend years trying to figure out the answer to a particular problem. To explain your discoveries to other people, you need to be able to write and speak in a clear, interesting way. You can learn many of these skills with the proper education and training.

If you want to become an astronomer, you need an education concentrating on mathematics, physics, and computer science. In North America, most astronomers get a Bachelor of Science (B.S.) degree in a physical science or mathematics. Then they attend graduate school for 5 to 7 years to get a Doctor of Philosophy (Ph.D.) degree in astronomy. Once an astronomer has a Ph.D., he or she does research and hopes to find a permanent job as a university teacher or researcher.

Studying outer space takes creativity and dedication. Sometimes it takes years to make a new discovery.

What are supernovas and quasars?

Supernovas are exploding stars. They usually occur when very large stars burn out. Supernovas are 100 million times brighter than the Sun. When a supernova has finished exploding, it becomes a white dwarf, which is a small star that is not very bright. When a star uses all its gases, its core is a huge ball of iron, about half the size of Earth. This core collapses in seconds to a ball just 6 miles (10 km) across. This releases a huge amount of energy, which blows the star apart. Through a telescope, quasars look just like stars. But quasars are billions of light years away. They are very small, but they put out more light and more radio waves than entire galaxies.

One theory about quasars is that each has an enormous black hole at its center, and that the light and energy are given off by matter falling into the black hole. Since many galaxies, including the Milky Way, probably have similar giant black holes at their centers, many scientists think quasars are the active centers of galaxies too far away to see.

The Crab Nebula is the remains of a supernova. The star exploded about 1,000 years ago. Early astronomers in Asia and the Middle East would have been able to see the explosion.

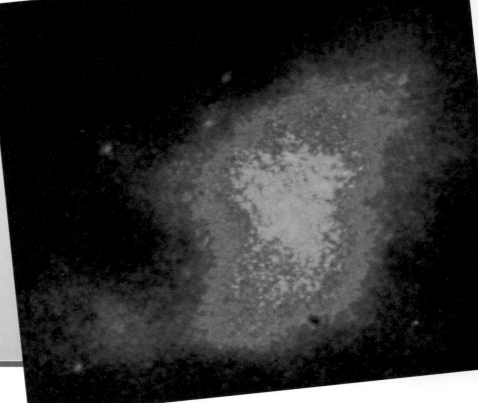

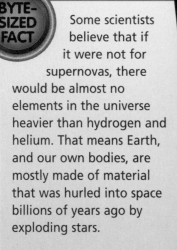

BYTE-SIZED FACT Some scientists believe that if it were not for supernovas, there would be almost no elements in the universe heavier than hydrogen and helium. That means Earth, and our own bodies, are mostly made of material that was hurled into space billions of years ago by exploding stars.

How Has the Study and Exploration of Space Helped People?

Studying and exploring space tells us more about our planet and its environment, our solar system, and the universe. We learn how our planet evolved and how we can take better care of it.

Space technologies have also led to many new technologies we use on Earth. Artificial satellites transmit phone calls and television signals around the world, monitor the weather and the environment, and help boats and airplanes make it safely to their destinations. Technology invented to help humans travel in space has improved medical treatment, computers, airplanes, cars, and other things on Earth.

It is also human nature to explore. Humans have always wanted to see what is over the horizon or in the next valley.

That is why humans have spread all over the planet, from the frozen reaches of the Arctic to the steamy jungles of the Amazon. Now that much of Earth has been explored, people are looking for a new frontier, the greatest of which is the one we look up into each night. Who knows what great discoveries await among those twinkling lights?

Space exploration has come a long way. Further exploration is only limited by human imagination.

Science Survey

Imagine you have the opportunity to plan and build a space station that will orbit around Earth, where ordinary people can live and work. There are many things to consider in your plans. For example, you would have to decide what types of food to take, how you would remove waste, and how to have a constant supply of clean freshwater. Do some brainstorming by yourself, or with your friends or family. Try to think of the things you would need to have on your space station. Then answer the survey questions on page 41.

What are your answers?

1. List as many things as you can think of that you would need to survive in space. Remember the things that we take for granted here on Earth but that are essential to our survival.

2. What types of food would you need to produce on your space station? Would there be anything that you would have to transport from Earth?

3. What would you do with all of the garbage and waste that would be produced on your space station? Try to think of some ways to reuse and recycle items that would normally be thrown out on Earth. (Remember, you cannot throw any garbage into space.)

4. What would you do if there were an emergency on your space station? How would you be prepared to get everybody safely back to Earth?

5. Who would you need to work on your space station? Think of some of the people who would help you keep things running smoothly.

6. Where would the power for your space station come from?

Eating in space can be a challenge. How would you plan to serve meals on a space station without all the food floating away?

Fast Facts

1. The Space Shuttle travels at approximately 5 miles (8 km) per second.

2. Food tastes different in space. Some astronauts find that in space, they hate to eat the foods that they normally like on Earth.

3. Before there were human astronauts, there were animal astronauts. For example, the United States sent a chimpanzee named Ham into space on January 31, 1961, and brought him safely back to Earth.

4. The Sun is so much bigger than the planets that it contains 99 percent of the solar system's total mass.

5. When a comet approaches the Sun, its tail is following it, but when it moves away from the Sun, its tail is in front of it!

6. The Milky Way galaxy is so big that light, traveling at 186,000 miles (300,000 km) per second, still takes 75,000 years to travel from one side of the galaxy to the other.

7. The universe contains about 50 billion galaxies.

8. You can tell how hot a star is by its color. Blue stars are hotter than yellow stars, which are hotter than red stars.

9. Alpha Centauri is one of the closest stars to Earth. But even at the speed of a jet airplane it would take you more than 9 million years to reach it!

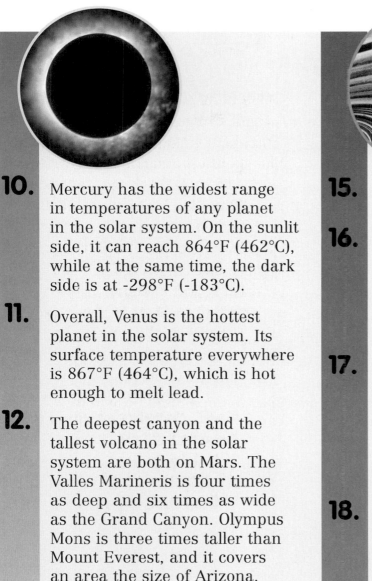

10. Mercury has the widest range in temperatures of any planet in the solar system. On the sunlit side, it can reach 864°F (462°C), while at the same time, the dark side is at -298°F (-183°C).

11. Overall, Venus is the hottest planet in the solar system. Its surface temperature everywhere is 867°F (464°C), which is hot enough to melt lead.

12. The deepest canyon and the tallest volcano in the solar system are both on Mars. The Valles Marineris is four times as deep and six times as wide as the Grand Canyon. Olympus Mons is three times taller than Mount Everest, and it covers an area the size of Arizona.

13. More than 3,000 asteroids have been discovered, mostly in the Asteroid Belt, which orbits the Sun between Mars and Jupiter.

14. When Neil Armstrong stepped onto the surface of the Moon, he said, "That's one small step for a man, one giant leap for mankind." The first words he actually said after he climbed out of the spacecraft and before he stepped onto the Moon were, "OK, Houston, I'm on the porch."

15. The Sun loses 8 million tons of gas every 2 seconds.

16. The word *astronaut* means "star voyager." It was chosen partly because of its similarity to aeronaut, or "sky voyager," which is what balloonists were called in the 1700s.

17. If your school were located on the Moon, it would take you 4 months, 29 days, 6 hours, and 10 minutes to get there on your school bus if you were traveling at a constant speed of 65 miles per hour (100 kph).

18. The brightest star in the sky is Sirius, located in the Canis Major constellation. It is sometimes called the "Dog Star."

19. One day on Venus is longer than 1 year on Venus! It turns on its axis once every 243 Earth days, but it takes only 225 days to go around the Sun once.

20. The light from the most distant galaxies that the Hubble Space Telescope can see has been traveling for 12 billion to 14 billion years by the time it reaches us.

FACT: The Moon appears to change shape at different times of the month. This change happens because of the changes in the Moon's position in its orbit around Earth, and because of its relationship to the Sun's light. You can demonstrate this change by using simple objects that you have at home.

TEST: While sitting in a darkened room, have a friend or family member hold a ball at different positions around a lamp or other light source. From where you are sitting, what are the differences in the illumination of the Moon at each point around the lamp? Does the shape of the lighted area change depending on where the ball is held?

FACT: Long ago, before television, video games, and computers, people told stories about the "pictures" they saw in the night sky. Many star groups were named for the people, animals, and objects our ancestors imagined when they looked at the stars.

You might want to look in the night sky for *Ursa Major*, also called the Big Dipper or Great Bear. *Ursa Minor*, also known as the Little Dipper or Little Bear, is not usually too far away.

TEST: Use your imagination and some art supplies to create pictures and stories of the star patterns you see in the night sky. You might even want to make up names for the shapes you see in the stars.

Research on Your Own

Do you know where to find information about space? Try your local library to find books about astronomy and space exploration. The Internet has some great websites about what is going on right now in astronomy and astronautics.
Check out these cool books and space sites!

Great Books

Asimov, Isaac. *Astronomy Today.* Milwaukee: Gareth Stevens, 1990.

Kerrod, Robin. *The Night Sky.* Tarrytown, NY: Benchmark Books, 1996.

Shedden, Robert. *Space.* New York: Chelsea House, 1996.

Time-Life Books. *Stars and Planets.* Alexandria, VA: Time-Life Books, 1996.

Great Websites

Ask an Astronaut
http://www.nss.org/askastro/

Astronomy for Kids
http://tqjunior.advanced.org/3645

Kennedy Space Center Home Page
http://www.ksc.nasa.gov/ksc.html

Views of the Solar System
http://www.hawastsoc.org/solar/homepage.htm

Glossary

asteroid: Any of the very small planets between Mars and Jupiter

atmosphere: The layer of air surrounding Earth

atom: The smallest particle of an element retaining all characteristics of that element

axis: The imaginary line that runs through the center of Earth

basalt: A type of rock that is very dark in color

black hole: A region in space produced by the collapse of a star

gravity: A force of attraction that draws two objects together

light year: The distance traveled by light in one year

magnetic field: The force around a magnet

mass: The amount of matter in an object

matter: The substance that an object is made of

meteor: A small particle of matter in the solar system

meteorite: A meteor that reaches Earth before burning up in the atmosphere

methane: A type of colorless gas

northern lights: The bands of light that sometimes appear in the northern sky at night

organic compounds: Chemicals that contain the element carbon, and are found in living things

oxidizer: A chemical that provides a source of oxygen

ozone: The gas that forms a layer of the atmosphere. Ozone absorbs ultraviolet radiation from the Sun and protects Earth.

phase: The shape of the Moon as it is seen at a given time

solar wind: The flow of gases given off by the Sun into space

sulfuric acid: A colorless, oily, strong acid

ultraviolet: A type of invisible radiation that is given off by the Sun

vacuum: Space that contains no matter

Index